English
Rapid Tests 2

Siân Goodspeed

Schofield&Sims

Introduction

This book gives you practice in answering English questions quickly.

The questions are like the questions on the 11+ and other school selection tests. You must find the correct answers.

School selection tests are usually timed, so you need to get used to working quickly. Each test has a target time for you to work towards. You should time how long you spend on each test, or you can ask an adult to time you.

What you need

- A pencil
- An eraser
- A clock, watch or stopwatch

- An adult to help you work out how long you take and to mark the test for you

What to do

- Turn to **Section 1 Test 1** on page 4. Look at the grey box at the top of the page labelled **Target time**. This tells you how long the test should take.

- When you are ready to start, write down the time or start the stopwatch. Or the adult helping you will tell you to begin.

- Read each question carefully and then write the answer on the answer line. Sometimes you need to tick or underline the correct answer instead.

- Try to answer every question. If you do get stuck on a question, leave it and go on to the next one. Work quickly and try your best.

- Each test is two pages long. When you reach the end, stop. Write down the time or stop the stopwatch. Or tell the adult that you have finished.

- With the adult, work out how long you took to do the test. Fill in the **Time taken** box at the end of the test.

- The adult will mark your test and fill in the **Score** and **Target met?** boxes.

- Turn to the **Progress chart** on page 40. Write your score in the box and colour in the graph to show how many questions you got right.

- Did you get some questions wrong? You should always have another go at them before you look at the answers. Then ask the adult to check your work and help you if you are still not sure.

- Later, you will do some more of these tests. You will soon learn to work through them more quickly. The adult who is helping you will tell you what to do next.

Published by **Schofield & Sims Ltd**,
7 Mariner Court, Wakefield, West Yorkshire WF4 3FL, UK
Telephone 01484 607080
www.schofieldandsims.co.uk

This edition copyright © Schofield & Sims Ltd, 2018
First published in 2018

Author: **Siân Goodspeed**. Siân Goodspeed has asserted her moral rights under the Copyright, Designs and Patents Act, 1988, to be identified as the author of this work. Any text not otherwise attributed has been written by Siân Goodspeed and is copyright © Schofield & Sims Ltd, 2018.

Daddy Fell into the Pond (page 10) is an extract from Daddy Fell into the Pond, and other poems for children by Alfred Noyes. Permission granted by The Society of Authors as the Literary Representative of the Estate of Alfred Noyes. **The New Adventures of Mr Toad: A Race for Toad Hall** (page 16) is an extract from THE NEW ADVENTURES OF MR TOAD: A RACE FOR TOAD HALL by Moorhouse (2017). 275w from pp. 102, 103 & 105. By permission of Oxford University Press. **The Worst Witch** (page 28) is an extract from THE WORST WITCH Copyright © 1974 by Jill Murphy, published by Puffin Books.

British Library Cataloguing in Publication Data. A catalogue record for this book is available from the British Library.

Design by **Ledgard Jepson Ltd**
Front cover design by **Ledgard Jepson Ltd**
Printed in the UK by **Page Bros (Norwich) Ltd**

ISBN 978 07217 1430 1

Contents

A **pull-out answers section** (pages A1 to A12) appears in the centre of this book, between pages 20 and 21. It also gives simple guidance on how best to use this book. Remove this section before the child begins working through the tests.

Read the text and answer the questions below.

GUINEA PIG JOINS NEW ZEALAND POLICE FORCE!

There has been a surprise new recruit in the New Zealand police force this month. Elliot the guinea pig has joined the force to help raise local awareness of a number of issues,
5 including road safety.

Constable Elliot has his own police uniform and has been posting comments on the New Zealand police's social media page.

Giving advice on safe driving, Elliot posted,
10 "I am not too fast and that's the way I like it – slow is safe! Keep this in mind when you are driving near any schools tomorrow. Remember people, the kids are going to be out and about walking and biking, and
15 crossing roads. Like me, they are small and unpredictable, so you have to watch out!"

Other social media posts show Elliot giving advice on stopping car theft and helping to answer the phones over the
20 busy Easter weekend.

Following the posts, Elliot has become something of a star, with thousands of likes on social media, and newspapers all around the world reporting on this unusual
25 police officer.

For any concerned animal lovers out there: don't worry – the New Zealand police force has reassured the public that Elliot is a very well cared-for guinea pig. When not busy
30 preventing crime, Elliot lives with a member of the police force. He is a sociable guinea pig who loves cuddles and enjoys eating his greens.

Write **A**, **B**, **C** or **D** on the answer line.

1. What is unusual about the New Zealand police force's recent recruit?
    A He is a dog.
    B He is a guinea pig.
    C He is a cat.
    D He is a rabbit.

    _____   /1

2. Why has Elliot joined the police force?
    A to catch criminals
    B there was a shortage of police officers
    C to encourage road safety
    D he wanted to drive a police car

    _____   /1

3. How has Elliot been giving people advice?
    A by posting on social media
    B by visiting people's homes
    C by speaking to prisoners
    D by writing in the newspapers

    _____   /1

4. Where does Elliot live?
    A at the police station
    B with a member of the police force
    C in a school
    D in a car

    _____   /1

5. Which <u>two</u> important messages has Elliot been giving the public? Tick the boxes.

Drive slowly near schools. ☐   Look after your pets. ☐   Keep children safe on the roads. ☐   Always drive at top speed. ☐

/2

6. Name <u>two</u> other things Elliot has done to help the police force.

_____

_____

/2

7. In what ways has Elliot become 'something of a star'?

_____

_____

/2

8. What <u>two</u> things does Elliot enjoy doing when he is not helping the police?

_____ and _____

/2

9. Why do you think the police force decided to use a guinea pig to get their message across?

_____

_____

_____

_____

/4

10. The passage below has had some words removed. Choose the correct words from the box. Write the missing words on the lines. You may use each word only once.

type	squeal	hutch	noises
mammal	carnivores	guinea pig	food
mouse	herbivores	vegetables	claws

Guinea pigs are a **a)** _____ of small rodent. They are

b) _____, which means that they eat only fruit and

c) _____. There are many breeds of **d)** _____

and they can be a variety of colours. Guinea pigs make lots of **e)** _____,

ranging from a soft, chirruping sound to a high-pitched **f)** _____.

/6

Score: _____   **Time taken:** _____   **Target met?** _____

Target time: **12 minutes**

1. Read the sentences below. Underline the correct verb form in each set of brackets.

   Example: Yesterday, I was (<u>jumping</u>   jumped   jumps) high on my trampoline.

   a) My favourite crisps (is   are   am) salt and vinegar flavour.

   b) Where (was   are   were) you yesterday?

   c) Lena's mother (taught   teached   teach) her how to knit.

   d) Elijah has (taken   took   takes) his dog to the vet's.

   /4

2. Read the sentences below. Underline the correct conjunction in each set of brackets.

   Example: I like school (if   and   <u>but</u>) I don't like homework!

   a) Pass me the salt (although   so   if) I can put some on my chips.

   b) You must eat up all your dinner (before   after   and) you can have your pudding.

   c) Samuel stayed home from school (although   yet   because) he was poorly.

   d) Lucia watched television (while   however   so) her father was cleaning the bathroom.

   /4

3. Write out each phrase on the line, using an apostrophe to show possession.

   Example: the house of the girl   <u>the girl's house</u>

   a) the jumper belonging to the old man   _____

   b) the wheels of the truck   _____

   c) the children of my neighbour   _____

   d) the den belonging to the fox   _____

   /4

4. Each sentence below is missing <u>two</u> items of punctuation. Write out each sentence on the line, adding in the correct sentence punctuation.

    Example: my brother is older than me   <u>My brother is older than me.</u>

    a) Her first name is marcia

    _____

    b) would you like milk in your tea

    _____

    c) that is so amazing

    _____

    d) how many birds can you see

    _____

    e) My best friends are Jacob Milo Luke and Neal.

    _____

    f) I asked sanjay if i could be his partner.

    _____

    /6

5. In each of the sentences below, <u>two</u> of the words have swapped places. Work out which words need to be swapped for the sentence to make sense. Underline the two words.

    Example: The meal <u>expensive</u> very <u>was</u>.

    a) It is a very day windy.

    b) The in is shining sun the sky.

    c) There were five pond on the ducklings.

    d) She piano her passed exam.

    /4

Score:	Time taken:	Target met?

1. Underline the word in each set of brackets that is closest in meaning to the word in bold.

   Example: cold   (hot <u>chilly</u> dry)

   a) caught   (fish net trapped)

   b) tiny   (massive minute grow)

   c) amazement   (gasp surprise win)

   d) growth   (age shrink increase)

   /4

2. Decide which of the words in bold is the correct word for each sentence. Underline the word.

   Example: I watched the **plain / <u>plane</u>** take off.

   a) He felt very **week / weak** after his long illness.

   b) I only have one clean **pair / pear** of socks left.

   c) Stanley wanted to **die / dye** his hair pink.

   d) We were excited to **meet / meat** the queen.

   /4

3. Underline the word in each set of brackets that means the <u>opposite</u> of the word in bold.

   Example: up   (left yes <u>down</u>)

   a) remember   (learn forget regret)

   b) answer   (question right wrong)

   c) leave   (go out arrive)

   d) continue   (stop progress go)

   /4

Schofield & Sims

4. Write out each sentence below on the line, replacing the words in bold with a contraction. Remember your apostrophes!

Example: I **cannot** find my favourite T-shirt.   _I can't find my favourite T-shirt._

a) Harry **could not** yet climb to the highest branch of the apple tree.

_____

b) Mohsin says **he is** not in the mood to play football today.

_____

c) I **do not** think it has ever been hotter!

_____

d) Playing the cello is hard, but I think **I am** getting better.

_____

e) **What will** you do all day while I am on holiday?

_____

f) Tia was delighted that **she had** won the competition.

_____

/6

5. One word in each set does not go with the others. Underline this odd word out.

Example: small   tiny   mini   <u>large</u>

a) rhombus   circle   square   rectangle

b) pear   grape   fruit   apple

c) height   measure   length   width

d) imagine   dream   walk   wonder

/4

Score:		Time taken:		Target met?	

Target time: **12 minutes**

Read the text and answer the questions below.

Daddy Fell into the Pond, by Alfred Noyes

Everyone grumbled. The sky was grey.
We had nothing to do and nothing to say.
We were nearing the end of a dismal day,
And there seemed to be nothing beyond,
5 THEN
Daddy fell into the pond!

And everyone's face grew merry and bright,
And Timothy danced for sheer delight.
"Give me the camera, quick, oh quick!
10 He's crawling out of the duckweed."
Click!

Then the gardener suddenly slapped his knee,
And doubled up, shaking silently,
And the ducks all quacked as if they were daft
15 And it sounded as if the old drake laughed.

O, there wasn't a thing that didn't respond
WHEN
Daddy fell into the pond!

Write **A**, **B**, **C** or **D** on the answer line.

1. What kind of afternoon was it?
   A a sunny afternoon
   B a dull afternoon
   C a stormy afternoon
   D a snowy afternoon

   _____ /1

2. Why did everyone grumble?
   A They were tired.
   B They were hungry.
   C They were sad.
   D They were bored.

   _____ /1

3. Who 'danced for sheer delight'?
   A Timothy
   B the gardener
   C Thomas
   D Mummy

   _____ /1

4. What did the gardener do?
   A fell over
   B laughed out loud
   C slapped his knee
   D took a photograph

   _____ /1

5. Which <u>two</u> adjectives best describe the children's feelings when their father falls into the pond? Tick the boxes.

uninterested ☐   miserable ☐   amused ☐   afraid ☐   excited ☐

/2

6. What did somebody take a photograph of?

_____

_____

/2

7. What was happening to the gardener when he 'doubled up, shaking silently'?

_____

_____

/2

8. Find a word in the poem that rhymes with each word below:

a) laughed _____   **b)** bright _____

/2

9. Describe how the mood of the poem changes from verse 1 to verse 2.

_____

_____

_____

_____

/4

10. The words on the left in blue can all be found in the poem. Draw lines to match each word with its meaning in the poem.

grumbled   silly

dismal   glee

merry   moaned

sheer   pure

delight   cheerful

daft   gloomy

/6

| Score: | | Time taken: | | Target met? | |

1. The words in each sentence below have been jumbled up and an extra word has been added that is not needed. Unjumble the sentence in your head so it makes sense and write the extra word on the line.

    Example: I like don't and cheese   _and_

    a) cheetahs like no I.   _____

    b) football loves She pitch playing.   _____

    c) pie Do apple you if like?   _____

    d) There dog bark are breeds many of.   _____

    e) It weekend the when is nearly.   _____

    f) after February January month comes.   _____

    /6

2. The sentences below are missing their speech marks. Write out each sentence on the line, adding the missing speech marks in the correct places.

    Example: Ava asked, Where are you going?   _Ava asked, "Where are you going?"_

    a) Don't move a muscle! shouted Billy.

    _____

    b) What's your name? asked the boy.

    _____

    c) The lady cried, Look out!

    _____

    d) Oh no he didn't! laughed the clown.

    _____

    /4

Schofield & Sims

3. Choose the correct word, **a** or **an**, to complete each sentence. Write it on the line.

Example: Sarah bought _a_ new hat.

a) It was _____ very hot day.

b) I'd like _____ orange, please.

c) We travelled to Spain in _____ aeroplane.

d) That is _____ great idea!

/4

4. Choose the best word, **when**, **before**, **after** or **while**, to complete each sentence. Write it on the line. You may use each word only once.

Example: I like playing outdoors _when_ the weather is hot.

a) I always brush my teeth _____ going to bed.

b) Tyler was scared _____ he heard the loud bang.

c) It is not wise to swim just _____ eating.

d) The grass grew very long _____ we were away.

/4

5. Underline the adjective in each sentence.

Example: The theatre trip was really <u>fun</u>.

a) Ruby thought her sister was very annoying.

b) The elephants at the zoo were massive.

c) "Thank you for being so helpful, Lucas," said his mother, quietly.

d) We will wear our glamorous outfits to the party.

/4

Score:		Time taken:		Target met?	

Target time: **12 minutes**

1. One word from the first set of brackets goes together with one word from the second set of brackets to make a new word. Underline the two words and write the new word on the line.

    Example: (<u>tooth</u> mouth nose)   (pen <u>brush</u> pencil)   <u>toothbrush</u>

    a) (leg foot arm)   (sleeve wave print)   _____

    b) (up out round)   (wall door roof)   _____

    c) (no yes is)   (sea sail land)   _____

    d) (nest tree egg)   (twig shell branch)   _____

    /4

2. Underline the word in each set of brackets that is closest in meaning to the word in bold.

    Example: cold   (hot <u>chilly</u> dry)

    a) **often**   (never frequently quickly)

    b) **probably**   (properly certain likely)

    c) **mischievous**   (clever naughty sensible)

    d) **accident**   (mishap rescue break)

    /4

3. One word in each set does not go with the others. Underline this odd word out.

    Example: small tiny mini <u>large</u>

    a) potatoes carrots turnips strawberries

    b) lorry car bicycle van

    c) hare pigeon squirrel mouse

    d) bench table chair stool

    /4

Schofield & Sims

4. Add **–ed** or **–ing** to the word in brackets so that each sentence makes sense. Write the new word on the line.

> **Example:** Last weekend, I (stay) at my aunt's house   _stayed_

a) My sister is (play) in a football match tomorrow.   _____

b) Our flight was (delay) by two hours.   _____

c) "Are you still (tidy) your room?" asked Dad.   _____

d) "I've nearly finished!" Edie (reply).   _____

e) Mavis reluctantly (empty) the dustbin.   _____

f) The fountain was (spray) the garden.   _____

/6

5. Write out the words in each row on the line so that they are in alphabetical order.

> **Example:** duck cat dog fox   _cat   dog   duck   fox_

a) egg toast butter jam

_____

b) prince queen princess king

_____

c) loud soft sound light

_____

d) six four five seven

_____

/4

Score:		Time taken:		Target met?	

Target time: **12 minutes**

Read the text and answer the questions below.

Extract from **The New Adventures of Mr Toad: A Race for Toad Hall, by Tom Moorhouse**

The loudspeakers crackled. "And now it's the event you've all been waiting for, the highlight of the day: it's the legendary Four-Fifteen at Pipergate! Ten laps of our track, and the fastest wins. So, ladies and gentlemen, take your places at the stands."
The crowd's cheer was loud even down by the track.
5 "This is it," said Teejay. "Are you ready, Mr T?"
"Just a moment." Mr Toad put on his driving helmet and goggles. "How do I look?"
"Not even slightly silly."
"Did all these people really come just to see me?"
"Oh yes," Teejay lied. "They heard that the best driver in the universe is here."
10 "Well, perhaps not the *whole* universe," said Mr Toad, humbly. He put on his gloves. "Righty-ho! Let us give my public what they want."
"Here they come!" shouted the loudspeakers. The crowd clapped as the drivers walked out, with Mr Toad in the lead.
He raised his arms and shouted, "Poop-poop!"
15 "What's that green thing?" called someone from the crowd.
"Dunno," said another. "Looks like a frog in a funny hat."
"Is it a frog or a toad?"
"Either way it'll be a ribbetting race."
Teejay winced, hoping Mr Toad had not heard. But he was busy posing. The last driver to walk out got
20 the biggest cheer. He wore white overalls. His crash-helmet was white, with blue glass that hid his face.
He went straight towards his sports car.
"Who's that chap?" said Mr Toad.
"That's Stiggy," said Teejay. "He's the stoat you have to beat."
"Why's he wearing that silly costume?"
25 Teejay glanced at Mr Toad's helmet and goggles. "Come on, let's find your car."

Write **A**, **B**, **C** or **D** on the answer line.

1. What event is taking place in the text?
    A a horse race
    B a cycle race
    C a motor car race
    D a running race

    _____ /1

2. How many laps of the track do they have to do?
    A one
    B ten
    C five
    D twenty

    _____ /1

3. In line 2, what time does it say the race is taking place?
    A 4.30 p.m.
    B 1.15 p.m.
    C 6.25 p.m.
    D 4.15 p.m.

    _____ /1

4. Who is about to race?
    A Mr Toad
    B Teejay
    C ladies
    D gentlemen

    _____ /1

5. What <u>two</u> items of protective clothing does Mr Toad put on?

_____ and _____   /2

6. Who was the first driver to walk out on to the track?

_____

_____   /2

7. Look at line 18. Why does someone in the crowd say, "... it'll be a ribbetting race"?

_____

_____   /2

8. Which driver was the crowd most excited to see?

_____

_____   /2

9. What does Teejay think of Mr Toad's outfit? Explain your answer.

_____

_____

_____

_____   /4

10. The words on the left in blue can all be found in the text. Draw lines to match each word with its meaning in the text.

highlight	the best part of something
legendary	pulled a face
slightly	a little bit
winced	standing in a particular way to impress others
posing	looked quickly
glanced	extremely well known

/6

Score:		Time taken:		Target met?	

Target time: **12 minutes**

1. In each of the sentences below, <u>two</u> of the words have swapped places. Work out which words need to be swapped for the sentence to make sense. Underline the two words.

   Example: The meal <u>expensive</u> very <u>was</u>.

   a) It today raining is.

   b) My is colour favourite blue.

   c) I won a the in teddy raffle.

   d) They long a very walked way.

/4

2. The passage below contains no punctuation. Write out the passage on the lines, adding in the correct punctuation.

everyone knew that a very grumpy giant lived in the castle high up in the clouds it was a creepy old castle and nobody usually dared to enter its tall gates is there anybody there said the young adventurer as he stepped cautiously into the castle the gloomy hallway was lined with dusty candlesticks long mirrors and sinister portraits

_____

_____

_____

_____

_____

_____

_____

/6

3. Read the sentences below. Underline the correct verb form in each set of brackets.

> **Example:** Yesterday, I was (<u>jumping</u> jumped jumps) high on my trampoline.

a) Last night, we were (dance dancing dances) on the stage.

b) Today, I am (drove drive driving) to the seaside.

c) Amy has (gone went going) home early.

d) Erin (sailing sail sails) every day.

/4

4. Underline the adverb in each sentence.

> **Example:** Macey <u>kindly</u> shared her toys with Leo.

a) We could not run quickly as we were so tired.

b) The children laughed loudly at the comedian's jokes.

c) "Stop teasing my brother!" the girl yelled angrily.

d) The cars drive fast around the racing track.

/4

5. Add in the missing apostrophes to the sentences below.

> **Example:** It is my sister's birthday tomorrow.

a) Has anyone seen Lucys pet hamster?

b) The giraffes baby had only just been born.

c) My grandfathers hat never leaves his head!

d) On Mondays, Mandips brother drives him to school.

/4

Score:		Time taken:		Target met?	

Target time: **12 minutes**

1. Write out the words in each row on the line so that they are in alphabetical order.

> **Example:** duck cat dog fox   <u>cat   dog   duck   fox</u>

a) coach   bus   lorry   car

_____

b) farm   barn   straw   field

_____

c) vest   robe   vain   rise

_____

d) straw   sour   shape   spare

_____

/4

2. Write out each sentence on the line, replacing the contraction in bold with two full words.

> **Example:** If you ask your teacher, **she'll** help you.
> <u>If you ask your teacher, she will help you.</u>

a) **There's** a new toy shop opening in the town centre.

_____

b) "Your grandparents said **they'll** pick you up after lunch," my dad told me.

_____

c) **Where's** the most interesting place you have ever visited?

_____

d) When **you've** finished eating your dinner, you can play outside.

_____

/4

English Rapid Tests 2 Answers

Notes for parents, tutors, teachers and other adult helpers

- **English Rapid Tests 2** is designed for seven- and eight-year-olds, but may also be suitable for some children of other ages.

- Remove this pull-out section before giving the book to the child.

- Before the child begins work on the first test, together read the instructions headed **What to do** on page 2. As you do so, point out to the child the suggested **Target time** for completing the test.

- Make sure the child has all the equipment in the list headed **What you need** on page 2.

- There are three sections in this book. Each section contains two comprehension tests, two grammar and punctuation tests, and two spelling and vocabulary tests.

- Explain to the child how he or she should go about timing the test. Alternatively, you may wish to time the test yourself. When the child has finished the test, together work out the **Time taken** and complete the box that appears at the end of the test.

- Mark the child's work using this pull-out section. Each test is out of 22 marks and each correct answer is worth one mark unless otherwise stated in the answers. Then complete the **Score** box at the end of the test.

- For all spelling questions, the answer must be spelt correctly for the full mark to be awarded. In the comprehension tests, the child does not need to write in full sentences for the marks to be awarded.

- This table shows you how to mark the **Target met?** box and the **Action** notes help you to plan the next step. However, these are suggestions only. Please use your own judgement as you decide how best to proceed.

Score	Time taken	Target met?	Action
1–11$\frac{1}{2}$	Any	Not yet	Give the child the previous book in the series. Provide help and support as needed.
12–17$\frac{1}{2}$	Any	Not yet	Encourage the child to keep practising using the tests in this book. The child may need to repeat some tests. If so, wait a few weeks or the child may simply remember the correct answers. Provide help and support as needed.
18–22	Over target – child took too long	Not yet	
18–22	On target – child took suggested time or less	Yes	Encourage the child to keep practising using further tests in this book, and to move on to the next book when you think this is appropriate.

- After finishing each test, the child should fill in the **Progress chart** on page 40.

- Whatever the test score, always encourage the child to have another go at the questions that he or she got wrong – without looking at the answers. If the child's answers are still incorrect, work through these questions together. Demonstrate the correct technique if necessary.

- If the child struggles with particular question types or areas, help him or her to develop the skills and strategies needed.

Answers

Section 1 Test 1 (pages 4–5)

1. B

2. C

3. A

4. B

5. Drive slowly near schools. and Keep children safe on the roads.

   Award 1 mark for each correctly ticked sentence. If more than two sentences are ticked, deduct 1 mark for every extra sentence ticked.

6. Elliot gave advice on stopping car theft and answered the phones over the Easter weekend.

   Award 1 mark for references to car theft prevention, and 1 mark for references to answering the phones.

7. He has become a star because newspapers around the world have reported his story and he has thousands of 'likes' on social media.

   Award 1 mark for references to 'likes' on social media, and 1 mark for references to being reported in newspapers.

8. cuddles and eating his greens

   Award 1 mark for references to cuddles, and 1 mark for references to him eating his greens/vegetables.

9. They used a guinea pig to grab people's attention and help get important messages across in an amusing way.

   Award 2 marks for answers that demonstrate that the child understands that the guinea pig was used to grab people's attention, and a further 2 marks for an explanation of why that might be, e.g. because it's funny/cute/amusing/unusual.

10. a) type
    b) herbivores
    c) vegetables
    d) guinea pig
    e) noises
    f) squeal

This question is testing the child's ability to make sense of a passage that is missing key words. To identify the correct words, they must pay attention to the meaning of the passage.

Section 1 Test 2 (pages 6–7)

1. a) are
   b) were
   c) taught
   d) taken

   This question is testing the child's understanding of singular/plural agreement (part **a**), verb tense (parts **b** and **c**), and the present perfect form (part **d**).

2. a) so
   b) before
   c) because
   d) while

   This question is testing the child's understanding of how subordinating conjunctions ('so', 'before', 'because', and 'while') link ideas in a sentence in different ways.

3. a) the old man's jumper
   b) the truck's wheels
   c) my neighbour's children
   d) the fox's den

   This question is testing the child's understanding of how to use apostrophes for possession. Make sure that the –'s is added to the correct noun in each case.

4. a) Her first name is **M**arcia**.**
   b) **W**ould you like milk in your tea**?**
   c) **T**hat is so amazing**!**
   d) **H**ow many birds can you see**?**
   e) **M**y best friends are Jacob**,** Milo**,** Luke and Neal.
   f) I asked **S**anjay if **I** could be his partner.

   This question is testing the child's ability to spot missing punctuation. Part **a** tests capitalisation of the first letter of a name and use of a full stop to end a sentence. Parts **b**, **c** and **d** test capitalisation of the first letter of a sentence and use of question marks/exclamation marks. Part **e** tests use of commas in a list. Part **f** tests capitalisation of names and of the pronoun 'I'. Award half a mark for each correctly inserted capital letter or punctuation mark.

5. **a)** day, windy

   b) in, sun

   c) pond, ducklings

   d) piano, passed

   This question is testing the child's knowledge of correct word order. Both correct words must be underlined in order for the mark to be awarded.

Section 1 Test 3 (pages 8–9)

1. **a)** trapped

   b) minute

   c) surprise

   d) increase

   This question is testing the child's knowledge of synonyms.

2. **a)** weak

   b) pair

   c) dye

   d) meet

   This question is testing the child's ability to distinguish between common homophones.

3. **a)** forget

   b) question

   c) arrive

   d) stop

   This question is testing the child's knowledge of antonyms (opposites).

4. **a)** Harry **couldn't** yet climb to the highest branch of the apple tree.

   b) Moshin says **he's** not in the mood to play football today.

   c) I **don't** think it has ever been hotter!

   d) Playing the cello is hard, but I think **I'm** getting better.

   e) **What'll** you do all day while I am on holiday?

   f) Tia was delighted that **she'd** won the competition.

   This question is testing the child's ability to correctly use and spell contractions. The apostrophe must be in the right place for the mark to be awarded.

5. **a)** circle (all the others have four straight sides)

   b) fruit (all the others are types of fruit)

   c) measure (all the others are dimensions)

   d) walk (all the others are to do with your thoughts)

   This question is testing the child's vocabulary and their ability to identify common features of words in order to find the odd one out.

Section 1 Test 4 (pages 10–11)

1. B

2. D

3. A

4. C

5. amused and excited

   Award 1 mark for each correctly ticked word. If more than two words are ticked, deduct 1 mark for every extra word ticked.

6. Daddy crawling out of the pond, covered in duckweed.

   Award 1 mark for references to it being a photograph of Daddy, and 1 mark for references to him crawling out of the pond/ through the duckweed.

7. The gardener was laughing so hard that he was bent over.

   Award 1 mark for references to the fact that the gardener was laughing very hard, and 1 mark for references to his bent posture.

8. **a)** daft

   b) delight

Answers

9. In the first verse, it is a dull, boring day and everybody is fed up. Then, when Daddy falls into the pond, the mood changes to being more light-hearted, as everyone finds it very funny.

Award 2 marks for references to the fact that in the first verse, it is dull/boring/everyone is fed up, and a further 2 marks for references to the fact that in the second verse, the mood becomes more cheerful.

10.
grumbled — silly
dismal — glee
merry — moaned
sheer — pure
delight — cheerful
daft — gloomy

Section 1 Test 5 (pages 12–13)

1. **a)** no (I like cheetahs.)
    b) pitch (She loves playing football.)
    c) if (Do you like apple pie?)
    d) bark (There are many breeds of dog.)
    e) when (It is nearly the weekend.)
    f) month (February comes after January.)
    This question is testing the child's knowledge of correct word order.

2. **a)** "Don't move a muscle!" shouted Billy.
    b) "What's your name?" asked the boy.
    c) The lady cried, "Look out!"
    d) "Oh no he didn't!" laughed the clown.
    This question is testing the child's ability to use speech marks to show when direct speech begins and ends.

3. **a)** a
    b) an
    c) an
    d) a
    This question is testing the child's ability to identify when to use 'a' or 'an'. You could

explain to the child that we use 'a' before words beginning with a consonant sound and 'an' before words beginning with a vowel sound.

4. **a)** before
    b) when
    c) after
    d) while
    This question is testing the child's understanding of how subordinating conjunctions ('after', 'before', 'when' and 'while') link events in time within a sentence.

5. **a)** annoying
    b) massive
    c) helpful
    d) glamorous
    This question is testing the child's ability to identify adjectives in a sentence.

Section 1 Test 6 (pages 14–15)

1. **a)** footprint
    b) outdoor
    c) island
    d) eggshell
    This question is testing the child's knowledge of compound words.

2. **a)** frequently
    b) likely
    c) naughty
    d) mishap
    This question is testing the child's knowledge of synonyms.

3. **a)** strawberries (all the others are root vegetables)
    b) bicycle (all the others are powered by an engine)
    c) pigeon (all the others are mammals)
    d) table (all the others are furniture that you sit on)
    This question is testing the child's vocabulary and their ability to identify common features of words in order to find the odd one out.

4.
a) playing
b) delayed
c) tidying
d) replied
e) emptied
f) spraying

This question is testing the child's ability to identify the correct suffix, **–ed** or **–ing**, and add these to words ending in **–y**. Draw the child's attention to any inconsistencies. For example, the root word stays the same when 'tidy' becomes 'tidying', but changes when it becomes 'tidied'.

5.
a) butter egg jam toast
b) king prince princess queen
c) light loud soft sound
d) five four seven six

This question is testing the child's knowledge of alphabetical order.

Section 2 Test 1 (pages 16–17)

1. C

2. B

3. D

4. A

5. (driving) helmet and goggles
Award 1 mark for each item.

6. Mr Toad
This question tests the child's inference skills. Award 2 marks for the correct answer.

7. They are making a joke about the driver (Mr Toad) being a frog or a toad, because 'ribbet' is the sound that frogs and toads make.
Award 2 marks for an answer that demonstrates that the child understands that it is a joke or a pun about the sound frogs and toads make.

8. Stiggy or the stoat
This question tests the child's inference skills. Award 2 marks for the correct answer.

9. Teejay thinks Mr Toad looks silly, because he says, "Not even slightly silly" when Mr Toad asks him how he looks, which suggests that he does actually think he looks silly. He also glances at Mr Toad's goggles and helmet when Mr Toad asks why Stiggy is wearing "that silly costume".
Award 2 marks for answers suggesting that Teejay thinks Mr Toad looks silly/comical/ funny. Award an additional 2 marks for references either to the fact that Teejay was lying when he said that Mr Toad did not look silly, or to Teejay glancing at Mr Toad's goggles and helmet when Mr Toad asks why Stiggy is wearing a silly costume.

10. highlight ⟶ the best part of something

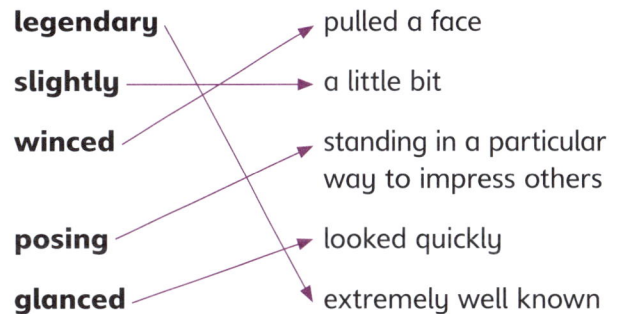

legendary — pulled a face

slightly — a little bit

winced — standing in a particular way to impress others

posing — looked quickly

glanced — extremely well known

Section 2 Test 2 (pages 18–19)

1.
a) today, is
b) is, favourite
c) the, teddy
d) long, walked

This question is testing the child's knowledge of correct word order. Both correct words must be underlined in order for the mark to be awarded.

2. Everyone knew that a very grumpy giant lived in the castle high up in the clouds. It was a creepy old castle and nobody usually dared to enter its tall gates. "Is there anybody there?" said the young adventurer as he stepped cautiously into the castle. The gloomy hallway was lined with dusty candlesticks, long mirrors and sinister portraits.

This question is testing the child's ability to make sense of a passage that is missing

Answers

Section 2 Test 2 (pages 18–19) continued

punctuation marks and to correctly insert the punctuation where needed. The parts in bold show where punctuation has been corrected/inserted. Award half a mark for each correctly inserted capital letter or punctuation mark. (Maximum 6 marks.)

3. **a)** dancing
   b) driving
   c) gone
   d) sails

   This question is testing the child's understanding of verb tense and verb–subject agreement. Remind the child that they can use time adverbs such as 'today' as clues to what tense they need to use.

4. **a)** quickly
   b) loudly
   c) angrily
   d) fast

   This question is testing the child's ability to identify adverbs in a sentence.

5. **a)** Has anyone seen Lucy**'**s pet hamster?
   b) The giraffe**'**s baby had only just been born.
   c) My grandfather**'**s hat never leaves his head!
   d) On Mondays, Mandip**'**s brother drives him to school.

   This question is testing the child's understanding of how to use apostrophes for possession. Make sure that the apostrophe is added to the correct noun in each case. In part **d**, there should not be an apostrophe in 'Mondays'.

Section 2 Test 3 (pages 20–21)

1. **a)** bus car coach lorry
   b) barn farm field straw
   c) rise robe vain vest
   d) shape sour spare straw

   This question is testing the child's knowledge of alphabetical order.

2. **a)** **There is** a new toy shop opening in the town centre.
   b) "Your grandparents said **they will** pick you up after lunch," my dad told me.
   c) **Where is** the most interesting place you have ever visited?
   d) When **you have** finished eating your dinner, you can play outside.

   This question is testing the child's ability to understand the meaning of common contractions.

3. **a)** impossible
   b) irregular
   c) uncertain
   d) incomplete
   e) discontinue
   f) dehydrate

   This question is testing the child's knowledge of forming opposites by adding appropriate prefixes.

4. **a)** hare
   b) bear
   c) tale
   d) hear

   This question is testing the child's ability to distinguish between common homophones.

5. **a)** road (all the others are buildings)
   b) skull (all the others are internal organs)
   c) string (all the others begin with the letter 'c')
   d) never (all the others mean something *could* happen)

   This question is testing the child's vocabulary and their ability to identify common features of words in order to find the odd one out.

Section 2 Test 4 (pages 22–23)

1. C

2. B

3. A

4. B

5. (small) rodents and birds

Award 1 mark for each item.

6. When they are born, kittens cannot see or hear.

Award 1 mark for references to sight, and 1 mark for references to hearing.

7. A cat's whiskers help it to sense objects and navigate in the dark.

Award 1 mark for references to sensing objects, and 1 mark for references to navigating in the dark.

8. Cats have better sight than humans.

This question tests the child's inference skills. Award 2 marks for a correct answer.

9. Yes, a cat has a good chance of surviving because they have a 'righting reflex' that enables them to twist in the air very quickly.

Award 2 marks for a positive response implying that a cat is very likely to survive, and a further 2 marks for referring to their reflexes or to twisting quickly and landing on their feet.

10. several ──────→ more than a few

vision ───→ sight

navigate ───→ find the way

athletic ───→ strong and fast

survival ───→ staying alive

reflex ───→ reaction

Section 2 Test 5 (pages 24–25)

1. **a)** "Watch out!" shouted the builder.

b) "What's your dog's name?" asked the vet.

c) Mum told Lizzie, "You'll be fine. You have done lots of practice."

d) "I think," said the teacher, "that it is time for lunch."

This question is testing the child's ability to use speech marks to show direct speech. In part **d**, both sets of speech marks need to be added in order for the mark to be awarded.

2.

Noun	Verb	Adjective	Adverb
chair	run	small	quickly
lion	sits	messy	lazily
rainbow	laughed	green	angrily
glove	hears	speckled	beautifully
girl	cycling	beautiful	gently

This question is testing the child's ability to assign words to different word classes. Award 1 mark for 4–7 correct words; 2 marks for 8–11 correct words; 3 marks for 12–15 correct words and 4 marks for 16 correct words. (Maximum 4 marks.) Note that 'green' and 'cycling' can also be nouns, but the answer given is the only way in which the table can be completed using each word only once.

3. **a)** flying

b) baked

c) thought

d) playing

This question is testing the child's understanding of verb tense and verb–subject agreement. Remind the child that they can use time adverbs, such as 'tomorrow', as clues to what tense they need to use.

4. **a)** through

b) in

c) across

d) over

e) inside

f) under

This question is testing the child's ability to identify prepositions. If the child struggles, you could remind them that a preposition tells us how one thing relates to another in terms of place, position or time.

5. **a)** an

b) an

c) a

d) an

This question is testing the child's ability to identify when to use 'a' or 'an'.

Answers

Section 2 Test 6 (pages 26–27)

1. a) disappear
    b) disagree
    c) unpopular
    d) unimportant

    This question is testing the child's knowledge of forming opposites by adding appropriate prefixes.

2. a) experiment
    b) strength
    c) sure
    d) lookout

    This question is testing the child's knowledge of synonyms.

3. a) moonlight
    b) wallpaper
    c) yourself
    d) knowledge

    This question is testing the child's knowledge of compound words.

4. a) piece
    b) ball
    c) real
    d) reins

    This question is testing the child's ability to distinguish between common homophones.

5.

Flowers	Fruit	Vegetables
daisy	apple	carrot
daffodil	nectarine	leek
lily	mango	cabbage
rose	melon	broccoli
tulip	banana	turnip

This question is testing the child's vocabulary and their ability to assign words to different categories. Award half a mark for each correctly identified word. (Maximum 6 marks.)

Section 3 Test 1 (pages 28–29)

1. D

2. B

3. A

4. D

5. The academy looked more like a prison than a school because of its gloomy grey walls and turrets.

    Award 1 mark for reference to gloomy grey walls, and 1 mark for reference to turrets.

6. Four from: (black) gymslips, (black) stockings, (black) hob-nailed boots, (grey) shirts, (black-and-grey) ties

    Award 1 mark for each correct item. (Maximum 4 marks.)

7. The sashes round their gymslips and the moon on the school badge were not black or grey.

    Award 1 mark for reference to the sashes round their gymslips, and 1 mark for reference to the school badge.

8. The pupils wore their robes and hats for prize-giving and Hallowe'en.

    Award 1 mark for each correct occasion.

9. Mildred's teachers were often annoyed when they saw her because she kept breaking the rules and her uniform was a mess.

    Award 1 mark for reference to Mildred breaking the rules, and 1 mark for reference to her messy uniform. Also award a mark for giving an example of what was wrong with Mildred's uniform. (Maximum 2 marks.)

10. Mildred's punishments were writing lines and being kept in.

    Award 1 mark for each correct punishment.

11. **Either:** No, I don't think Mildred had fun at the academy because it is dark and gloomy and it sounds very strict.

    Award 4 marks for answers giving two valid reasons. Possible reasons might include the dark and gloomy castle; it being a strict school;

Schofield & Sims

the rules and tests; Mildred getting into trouble; and Mildred being punished. If the child has only given one reason, award only 2 marks.

Or: Yes, I think Mildred did have fun at the academy, despite always getting into trouble, because she had lots of friends and a best friend who was loyal to her. They also did lots of fun activities such as flying on broomsticks and making potions.

Award 4 marks for answers giving two valid reasons. Possible reasons might include Mildred having lots of friends; Mildred having a loyal best friend; and doing fun activities such as flying on broomsticks and making potions. If the child has only given one reason, award only 2 marks.

Also award 4 marks for answers giving a valid reason for both 'no' and 'yes'.

Section 3 Test 2 (pages 30–31)

1. **a)** My name is **J**essica and **I** am eight.
    b) **W**hat time does the train leave**?**
    c) **"**What are you doing in here?**"** demanded the teacher.
    d) **"**It's not too far to go now,**"** said Asif.
    This question is testing the child's ability to spot missing punctuation. Part **a** tests capitalisation of the first letter of names and of the pronoun 'I'; part **b** tests capitalisation of the first letter in a sentence and use of question marks; and parts **c** and **d** test punctuation for direct speech. Award half a mark for each correctly inserted capital letter or punctuation mark.

2. **a)** insects
    b) live
    c) lays
    d) find
    e) protect
    f) job
    This question is testing the child's ability to make sense of a passage that is missing key words. To identify the correct words, they must pay attention to the verb endings, meaning and tense.

3. **a)** are (It's time for school.)
    b) he (My gran is 80 today.)
    c) hutch (I have two pet rabbits.)
    d) she (I eat dinner at 6.00 p.m.)
    This question is testing the child's knowledge of correct word order.

4. **a)** an
    b) a
    c) an
    d) an
    This question is testing the child's ability to identify when to use 'a' or 'an'. In part **d**, you could point out that although 'hour' starts with a consonant letter, it begins with a vowel sound, and so 'an' is used.

5. **a)** riding
    b) won
    c) swim
    d) went
    This question is testing the child's understanding of verb tense and verb–subject agreement. Remind the child that they can use time adverbs as clues to what tense they need to use.

Section 3 Test 3 (pages 32–33)

1. **a)** difficult, easy
    b) straight, bent
    c) join, separate
    d) positive, negative
    This question is testing the child's knowledge of antonyms (opposites).

2. **a)** watermelon
    b) drumstick
    c) blackbird
    d) newspaper
    This question is testing the child's knowledge of compound words.

Answers

Section 3 Test 3 (pages 32–33) continued

3. **a)** dislike (all the others are related to positive emotions)

    b) dull (all the others describe something remarkable)

    c) Wednesday (all the others are months of the year)

    d) stop (all the others indicate movement)

    This question is testing the child's vocabulary and their ability to identify common features of words in order to find the odd one out.

4. **a)** I complained that I **didn't** want to walk the dog.

    b) A herbivore is an animal that **doesn't** eat meat.

    c) Whilst **we're** in Paris, we will visit the Eiffel Tower.

    d) **What've** you read recently that you really enjoyed?

    e) If you practise every day, **you'll** soon be able to play the flute.

    f) Kai's friends, **who've** been fundraising for charity, are holding a cake sale.

    This question is testing the child's ability to correctly spell contractions. The apostrophe must be in the right place for the mark to be awarded.

5. **a)** sensibly

    b) specifically

    c) guiltily

    d) dramatically

    This question is testing the child's ability to add a suffix to an adjective to form an adverb. If the child struggles, remind them of the following rules: if the root word ends in **–le**, these two letters are replaced by **–ly**. If the root word ends in **–ic**, **–ally** is added rather than just **–ly**. If the root word ends in **–y**, **–ily** is added rather than just **–ly**.

Section 3 Test 4 (pages 34–35)

1. A

2. D

3. A

4. C

5. The author thinks you should only eat them occasionally because they contain a lot of sugar.

    Award 1 mark for answering that the treats should be eaten occasionally/sometimes/not every day, and 1 mark for stating that this is because of their sugar content.

6. chocolate buttons and butter

    Award 1 mark for each correct answer. Award only half a mark for 'melted chocolate'.

7. **a)** well

    b) command

    Award 1 mark for each correct answer. In part **b**, do not award the mark if more than one option has been ticked.

8. The best things are that it only takes 5 minutes and you can eat the ingredients as you make it.

    Award 1 mark for references to the recipe being quick to make, and 1 mark for references to being able to eat the ingredients whilst you are making it.

9. A serving suggestion is an idea for how you could present the bites.

    Award 2 marks for answers to this effect using the child's own words. Award only 1 mark for answers reusing the source words, for example 'A serving suggestion is a suggestion for how the bites should be served.'

10. **a)** me**asu**re

    b) dr**ied**

    c) proc**ess**or

    d) do**ugh**

    e) sun**flow**er

    f) sl**ice**s

    g) Fin**ally**

    h) rem**ain**ing

Section 3 Test 5 (pages 36–37)

1. **a)** that
    b) and
    c) because
    d) or

    This question is testing the child's understanding of how conjunctions ('that', 'and', 'because' and 'or') link things or events in a sentence.

2. **a)** the, love
    b) cricket, cousin
    c) languages, speak
    d) walk, the

    This question is testing the child's knowledge of correct word order. Both correct words must be underlined in order for the mark to be awarded.

3. **a)** the singer's voice
    b) the dog's dinner
    c) Sally's homework
    d) the orchestra's sound

    This question is testing the child's understanding of how to use apostrophes for possession. Make sure that the –'s is added to the correct noun in each case.

4.

Adjective	Noun	Preposition	Adverb
heavy	table	over	slowly
hungry	hill	below	bravely
grumpy	pond	by	easily
eager	apple	across	sleepily
lonely	horse	near	thankfully

This question is testing the child's ability to assign words to different word classes. Note that each preposition would be classed as an adverb when used in a sentence where it does not have an object, and 'near' can also be an adjective, but this is the only way in which the table can be completed using each word only once. Award 1 mark for 4–7 correct words;

2 marks for 8–11 correct words; 3 marks for 12–15 correct words and 4 marks for 16 correct words. (Maximum 4 marks.)

5. **C**harlotte said to her mother**,** "I LOVE cats**!** **P**lease**,** please**,** please can I have one**?**" **C**harlotte's mother told her she could have a cat if she was able to look after it herself**.** Charlotte was determined to prove that she would be a good cat owner**.**

    This question is testing the child's ability to identify when to use capital letters, commas, full stops, exclamation marks and question marks, as well as how to punctuate direct speech. Award half a mark for each correctly inserted capital letter or punctuation mark. In the first sentence, a full stop instead of an exclamation mark is also acceptable. (Maximum 6 marks.)

Section 3 Test 6 (pages 38–39)

1. **a)** middle
    b) own
    c) position
    d) plenty

    This question is testing the child's knowledge of synonyms.

2. **a)** break
    b) sew
    c) Where
    d) sole

    This question is testing the child's ability to distinguish between common homophones.

3. **a)** therefore
    b) timetable
    c) lifeline
    d) sunlight

    This question is testing the child's knowledge of compound words.

Section 3 Test 6 (pages 38–39) continued

4. **a)** branch leaf trunk twig

    b) car coach truck van

    c) clap clip creep crow

    d) feather feed fire free

    This question is testing the child's knowledge of alphabetical order.

5. favourite, sensation, tongue, flavour, delicious, raspberry

    Award 1 mark for each correct question part. Award only half a mark if the error has been underlined but not corrected accurately. Each correct spelling can be written on any of the answer lines for the mark to be awarded.

This book of answers is a pull-out section from **English Rapid Tests 2**.

Published by **Schofield & Sims Ltd**,
7 Mariner Court, Wakefield, West Yorkshire WF4 3FL, UK
Telephone 01484 607080
www.schofieldandsims.co.uk

This edition copyright © Schofield & Sims Ltd, 2018
First published in 2018

Author: **Siân Goodspeed**. Siân Goodspeed has asserted her moral rights under the Copyright, Designs and Patents Act, 1988, to be identified as the author of this work.

British Library Cataloguing in Publication Data. A catalogue record for this book is available from the British Library.

Design by **Ledgard Jepson Ltd**
Printed in the UK by **Page Bros (Norwich) Ltd**

ISBN 978 07217 1430 1

3. Add a prefix to the beginning of each word to change it into its opposite. Write the new word on the line.

Example: ____done ⟶ _undone_

a) ____possible ⟶ _____

b) ____regular ⟶ _____

c) ____certain ⟶ _____

d) ____complete ⟶ _____

e) ____continue ⟶ _____

f) ____hydrate ⟶ _____

/6

4. Decide which of the words in bold is the correct word for each sentence. Underline the word.

Example: I watched the **plain / plane** take off.

a) The **hair / hare** raced across the field.

b) The grizzly **bear / bare** caught a fish.

c) It was a magical **tail / tale** of adventure.

d) I didn't **hear / here** the doorbell ring.

/4

5. One word in each set does not go with the others. Underline this odd word out.

Example: small   tiny   mini   large

a) library   hospital   school   road

b) skull   heart   liver   kidney

c) cash   string   count   clip

d) perhaps   never   maybe   possibly

/4

Score:		Time taken:		Target met?	

Read the text and answer the questions below.

All About Cats

Cats are popular household pets. There are roughly 8 million cats in the UK*. There are many different breeds of cat, including the Siamese, British Shorthair, Ragdoll and Maine Coon. Cats live for around 12 to 15 years and usually weigh between four and five kilograms.

5 Cats spend much of their lives asleep, with the average cat sleeping up to 16 hours a day. When they are not sleeping, many cats enjoy exploring and hunting outside. They will often bring their owners little 'gifts' of small rodents or birds.

Baby cats are called kittens. Kittens are born in litters of two to five. When they are born, kittens' eyes are closed and their ears are folded down, so they are born blind and deaf. This is because their senses need some time to develop. Kittens' eyes and ears will usually open when they are between 5 and 14 10 days old. It takes several weeks before they can see and hear as well as an adult cat.

Adult cats have excellent hearing and a superior sense of smell. They also have very good night vision and can see in low light. A cat's whiskers help it to sense objects and to navigate in the dark.

Cats are athletic animals. They can run up to 30 miles per hour 15 and jump up very high. If a cat falls from a height, it has a very high chance of survival. This is because cats nearly always land on their feet. They are able to do this thanks to the 'righting reflex', which enables them to twist in the air very quickly so that they land safely.

*2017 estimated figures from the **Pet Food Manufacturers' Association (PFMA)**

Write **A**, **B**, **C** or **D** on the answer line.

1. Which of the following is <u>not</u> a breed of cat mentioned in the text?

   A Ragdoll

   B Maine Coon

   C Persian

   D Siamese

   _____ /1

2. How long do cats normally live for?

   A 5–10 years

   B 12–15 years

   C 20–30 years

   D 1–2 years

   _____ /1

3. Around how many cats are there in the UK?

   A 8 million

   B 10 million

   C 5.8 million

   D 8 billion

   _____ /1

4. What do cats spend much of their lives doing?

   A eating

   B sleeping

   C hunting

   D fighting

   _____ /1

5. What 'gifts' do cats often like to give their owners?

_____ or _____   /2

6. What <u>two</u> things can kittens not yet do when they are born?

_____

_____   /2

7. What do a cat's whiskers help it to do?

_____

_____   /2

8. Aside from their excellent hearing and sense of smell, which other sense is better in cats than in humans?

_____

_____   /2

9. Is a cat likely to survive if it falls from a height? Explain your answer.

_____

_____

_____

_____   /4

10. The words on the left in blue can all be found in the text. Draw lines to match each word with its meaning in the text.

several	more than a few
vision	strong and fast
navigate	reaction
athletic	sight
survival	staying alive
reflex	find the way

/6

Score:	Time taken:	Target met?

1. Add the missing speech marks to the sentences below. Watch out: some sentences may have more than one set of speech marks.

   Example: Louisa asked, "Where are you going?"

   a) Watch out! shouted the builder.

   b) What's your dog's name? asked the vet.

   c) Mum told Lizzie, You'll be fine. You have done lots of practice.

   d) I think, said the teacher, that it is time for lunch.

   /4

2. Sort each word in the word bank into the correct word class by writing it in the table below. You may use each word only once. The first row has been done for you.

   Word bank

sits	lion	lazily	~~chair~~
rainbow	green	~~run~~	messy
~~small~~	beautifully	laughed	angrily
speckled	~~quickly~~	glove	hears
girl	cycling	gently	beautiful

Noun	Verb	Adjective	Adverb
chair	run	small	quickly

   /4

3. Read the sentences below. Underline the correct verb form in each set of brackets.

Example: Yesterday, I was (<u>jumping</u> jumped jumps) high on my trampoline.

a) Tomorrow, I am (fly flying flies) to New York.

b) This morning, David (baked bakes baking) a cake.

c) I (think thought thinks) you had already left.

d) Jack was (plays played playing) the violin beautifully.

/4

4. Underline the preposition in each sentence.

a) The dog jumped eagerly through the hoop.

b) Omari carefully placed his sandwiches in his lunchbox.

c) The ballerina pirouetted across the stage.

d) Matty leapt gracefully over the wall.

e) Annette hid inside the wardrobe.

f) The sheep huddled together under the old oak tree.

/6

5. Choose the correct word, **a** or **an**, to complete each sentence. Write it on the line.

Example: Sarah bought _a_ new hat.

a) It's been _____ extremely busy week.

b) I saw _____ octopus at the aquarium.

c) A baby cow is called _____ calf.

d) Martin ate _____ egg and four pieces of toast for breakfast.

/4

Score:		Time taken:		Target met?	

1. Add a prefix to the beginning of each word to change it into its opposite. Write the new word on the line.

   Example: ____done ⟶ <u>undone</u>

   a) ____appear ⟶ _____

   b) ____agree ⟶ _____

   c) ____popular ⟶ _____

   d) ____important ⟶ _____

   /4

2. Underline the word in each set of brackets that is closest in meaning to the word in bold.

   Example: cold (hot <u>chilly</u> dry)

   a) **test** (expert experiment result)

   b) **power** (strength switch light)

   c) **certain** (confused sure decide)

   d) **guard** (tower dog lookout)

   /4

3. One word from the first set of brackets goes together with one word from the second set of brackets to make a new word. Underline the two words and write the new word on the line.

   Example: (<u>tooth</u> mouth nose) (pen <u>brush</u> pencil) <u>toothbrush</u>

   a) (dark shine moon) (light sky star) _____

   b) (floor wall door) (pen paper book) _____

   c) (you they your) (self name face) _____

   d) (know think feel) (happy ledge sad) _____

   /4

4. Decide which of the words in bold is the correct word for each sentence. Underline the word.

Example: I watched the **plain / <u>plane</u>** take off.

a) He ate a **piece / peace** of the birthday cake.

b) The dress was perfect for the **ball / bawl**!

c) She was surprised that the flowers were not **real / reel**.

d) The horse was pulling against its **reins / reigns**.

/4

5. Sort each word in the word bank into the correct category by writing it in the table below. The first row has been done for you.

Word bank

banana	daffodil	lily
turnip	~~carrot~~	tulip
melon	nectarine	~~apple~~
rose	broccoli	mango
~~daisy~~	cabbage	leek

Flowers	Fruit	Vegetables
daisy	apple	carrot

/6

Score:		Time taken:		Target met?	

Target time: **12 minutes**

Read the text and answer the questions below.

Extract from **The Worst Witch, by Jill Murphy**

Miss Cackle's Academy for Witches stood at the top of a high mountain surrounded by a pine forest. It looked more like a prison than a school, with its gloomy grey walls and turrets. Sometimes you could see the pupils on their broomsticks flitting like bats above the playground wall, but usually the place was half hidden in mist, so that if you had glanced up at the mountain you would probably not
5 have noticed the building was there at all.

Everything about the school was dark and shadowy, with long, narrow corridors and winding staircases – and of course there were the girls themselves, dressed in black gymslips, black stockings, black hob-nailed boots, grey shirts and black-and-grey ties. Even their summer dresses were black-and-grey checked. The only touches of colour were the sashes round their gymslips – a different colour for each
10 house – and the school badge, which was a black cat sitting on a yellow moon. For special occasions, such as prize-giving or Hallowe'en, there was another uniform consisting of a long robe worn with a tall, pointed hat, but as these were black too, it didn't really make much of a change.

There were so many rules that you couldn't do *anything* without being told off, and there seemed to be tests and exams every week.

15 Mildred Hubble was in her first year at the school. She was one of those people who always seem to be in trouble. She didn't exactly mean to break rules and annoy the teachers, but things just seemed to *happen* whenever she was around. You could rely on Mildred to have her hat on back-to-front or her bootlaces trailing along the floor. She couldn't walk from one end of a corridor to the other without someone yelling at her, and nearly every night she was writing lines or being kept in (not that there was
20 anywhere to go if you were allowed out). Anyway, she had lots of friends, even if they did keep their distance in the potion laboratory, and her best friend Maud stayed loyally by her through everything, however hair-raising.

Write **A**, **B**, **C** or **D** on the answer line.

1. Where was Miss Cackle's Academy for Witches?
   A on Witch Street
   B in a misty valley
   C in a dark cave
   D at the top of a mountain

   _____ /1

2. What could you sometimes see above the playground wall?
   A bats flying about
   B pupils on their broomsticks
   C owls swooping
   D nothing because of the mist

   _____ /1

3. Which words best describe the school?
   A dark and gloomy
   B bright and cheerful
   C airy and spacious
   D ornate and colourful

   _____ /1

4. What was Mildred's best friend called?
   A Miss Cackle
   B Hubble
   C Mary
   D Maud

   _____ /1

5. What made the academy look 'more like a prison than a school'?

_____

_____   /2

6. List <u>four</u> items of winter uniform worn by the pupils.

_____   _____

_____   _____   /4

7. Which parts of the school uniform were <u>not</u> black or grey?

_____

_____   /2

8. Name <u>two</u> occasions when the pupils would wear their long robes and pointed hats.

_____

_____   /2

9. Why do you think Mildred's teachers were often annoyed when they saw her in the corridors?

_____

_____   /2

10. Which <u>two</u> punishments did Mildred often receive?

_____

_____   /2

11. Do you think Mildred had fun at Miss Cackle's Academy for Witches? Give <u>two</u> reasons.

_____

_____

_____

_____   /4

Score:		Time taken:		Target met?	

1. Each sentence below is missing <u>two</u> items of punctuation. Write out the sentence on the line, adding in the correct sentence punctuation.

Example: my brother is older than me   <u>My brother is older than me.</u>

a) My name is jessica and i am eight.

_____

b) what time does the train leave

_____

c) What are you doing in here? demanded the teacher.

_____

d) It's not too far to go now, said Asif.

_____

/4

2. The passage below has had some words removed. Choose the correct word from the box. Write the missing word on the line. You may use each word only once.

made	protect	find	hive
living	insects	live	job
was	wasp	lays	protection

Bees are the only **a)** _____ that produce a food that humans

can eat – honey. Honey bees **b)** _____ in hives. There are three

types of bee in each hive: the queen, the workers and the drones. The queen bee

c) _____ the eggs that will produce the next generation of bees.

The workers are female bees, and their role is to **d)** _____ food

(pollen and nectar from flowers) and to build and **e)** _____ the hive.

Drones are male bees and it is their **f)** _____ to mate with the queen bee.

/6

3. The words in each sentence below have been jumbled up and an extra word has been added that is not needed. Unjumble the sentence in your head so it makes sense and write the extra word on the line.

Example: I like don't and cheese.   *and*

a) are It's for time school.   _____

b) 80 gran My is he today.   _____

c) rabbits I pet have hutch two.   _____

d) dinner I she eat 6.00 p.m. at.   _____

/4

4. Choose the correct word, **a** or **an**, to complete each sentence. Write it on the line.

Example: Sarah bought _a_ new hat.

a) It is _____ unusual bird.

b) Would you like _____ cake?

c) Millie was in _____ angry mood.

d) It takes _____ hour to get there.

/4

5. Read the sentences below. Underline the correct verb form in each set of brackets.

Example: Yesterday, I was (jumping   jumped   jumps) high on my trampoline.

a) I spend twenty minutes each day (riding   rode   rides) to school.

b) The youngest horse has (win   won   winning) the race.

c) My little brother cannot (swimming   swam   swim) yet.

d) Last week, I (gone   went   going) on holiday.

/4

Score:		Time taken:		Target met?	

Target time: **12 minutes**

1. Underline the two words (one in each set of brackets) that are <u>opposite</u> in meaning.

   Example: (<u>hot</u> chilly dry)   (fast slow <u>cold</u>)

   a) (over difficult old)   (easy hard last)

   b) (straight curved oval)   (long thin bent)

   c) (join split argue)   (pierce separate row)

   d) (sad positive happy)   (difficult good negative)

   /4

2. One word from the first set of brackets goes together with one word from the second set of brackets to make a new word. Underline the two words and write the new word on the line.

   Example: (<u>tooth</u> mouth nose)   (pen <u>brush</u> pencil)   <u>toothbrush</u>

   a) (leak drip water)   (banana pear melon)   _____

   b) (piano drum flute)   (twig stick branch)   _____

   c) (pink black green)   (bird penguin sparrow)   _____

   d) (story news old)   (paper card tissue)   _____

   /4

3. One word in each set does not go with the others. Underline this odd word out.

   Example: small tiny mini <u>large</u>

   a) favourite best preferred dislike

   b) dull unusual different special

   c) January November Wednesday February

   d) forward stop backward sideways

   /4

4. Write out each sentence below on the line, replacing the words in bold with a contraction. Remember your apostrophes!

Example: I **cannot** find my favourite T-shirt.   *I can't find my favourite T-shirt.*

a) I complained that I **did not** want to walk the dog.

_____

b) A herbivore is an animal that **does not** eat meat.

_____

c) Whilst **we are** in Paris, we will visit the Eiffel Tower.

_____

d) What have you read recently that you really enjoyed?

_____

e) If you practise every day, **you will** soon be able to play the flute.

_____

f) Kai's friends, **who have** been fundraising for charity, are holding a cake sale.

_____

_____

/6

5. Add the suffix **–ly** to each of the following words. You may have to make spelling changes. Write the new word on the line.

Example: merry   *merrily*

a) sensible   _____

b) specific   _____

c) guilty   _____

d) dramatic   _____

/4

Score:		Time taken:		Target met?	

Read the text and answer the questions below.

Recipe: Rocky Road Bites

Author's note

These are so yummy that you'll want to eat them every day! However, as they are very sugary, it is better to
5   enjoy them as an occasional treat.

Ingredients

- 1 mug mini marshmallows
- $1\frac{1}{2}$ mugs chocolate buttons
- 1 mug broken digestive biscuits
- 1 mug sultanas
- 35g butter

Method

Makes: 10 bites   Prep: 5 minutes   Extra time: 25 minutes chilling   Ready in: 30 minutes

1. Put the chocolate buttons and butter in a microwaveable dish and heat for about 35 seconds (or until melted).
10 2. Remove from the microwave and mix well.
3. Place the sultanas, biscuits and marshmallows in a bowl with the melted chocolate and butter.
4. Mix well, so that everything is coated.
5. Place the mixture in small dollops on to a foil-covered baking tray.
6. Put the tray into the fridge for about 25 minutes (or until set).

15 *Tasty tip*

You can add cherries and mess around with the amount of each ingredient to suit your own tastes. The best things about this recipe are that it only takes 5 minutes to prepare and most of the ingredients can be eaten at any point during the preparation time!

Serving suggestion

20 Best enjoyed chilled. These would be great as part of a midnight feast!

Write **A**, **B**, **C** or **D** on the answer line.

1. How many bites does the recipe make?

  A 10

  B 25

  C 15

  D 5

_____   /1

2. Which of the following is not an ingredient in the recipe?

  A chocolate buttons

  B sultanas

  C butter

  D flour

_____   /1

3. How should you melt the butter?

  A in the microwave

  B on the hob

  C in the sun

  D not at all

_____   /1

4. Altogether, how long does it take to prepare and chill the bites?

  A 5 minutes

  B 25 minutes

  C 30 minutes

  D 1 hour

_____   /1

5. Read lines 2–5. How often does the author think you should eat rocky road bites? Why?

_____

_____ /2

6. Which ingredients go into the microwaveable dish?

_____ and _____ /2

7. **a)** Look at this sentence from the text. Underline the adverb.

> Mix well, so that everything is coated.

b) What type of sentence is used in the 'Method' section? Tick <u>one</u> box.

> statement ☐   conditional ☐   command ☐   exclamation ☐   /2

8. What are the <u>two</u> 'best things' about making this recipe?

_____

_____ /2

9. In your own words, explain what 'serving suggestion' means.

_____

_____ /2

10. Here is the method for another recipe. The words in bold have some letters missing. Fill in the missing letters so that the text makes sense.

Recipe: Trail Mix Cookies

- Gather all the ingredients and **a)** **me** ___ ___ ___**re** them out.

- Place the oats, most of the desiccated coconut and the **b)** **dr** ___ ___ ___ fruit into a food

  c) **proc** ___ ___ ___ **or**.

- Process until the **d)** **do** ___ ___ ___ lifts away from the bowl's edge.

- Gently, knead in the **e)** **sunf** ___ ___ ___ **er** seeds.

- Form into a log shape and cut into 12 **f)** **sl** ___ ___ ___ **s**.

- **g)** **Fin** ___ ___ ___ **y**, roll each slice into the **h)** **rem** ___ ___ ___ **ing** coconut.   /8

Score:		Time taken:		Target met?	

1. Choose the best word, **that**, **or**, **because** or **and**, to complete each sentence. Write it on the line. You may use each word only once.

   Example: I eat fruit _because_ it is good for me.

   a) Did you hear me say _____ the food is too hot?

   b) Rats _____ mice are types of rodent.

   c) Enzo ate the last biscuit _____ he is greedy!

   d) Either Hazna _____ Ben won the race.

   /4

2. In each of the sentences below, <u>two</u> of the words have swapped places. Work out which words need to be swapped for the sentence to make sense. Underline the two words.

   Example: The meal <u>expensive</u> very <u>was</u>.

   a) I the singing in love rain!

   b) Her cricket plays cousin on Sundays.

   c) My sister can languages three speak.

   d) I missed walk bus so I had to the home.

   /4

3. Write out each phrase on the line, using an apostrophe to show possession.

   Example: the house of the girl _the girl's house_

   a) the voice of the singer _____

   b) the dinner belonging to the dog _____

   c) the homework that Sally did _____

   d) the sound of the orchestra _____

   /4

4. Sort each word in the word bank into the correct word class by writing it in the table below. You may use each word only once. The first row has been done for you.

Word bank

below	pond	~~heavy~~	thankfully
~~table~~	sleepily	lonely	eager
grumpy	across	near	~~over~~
apple	easily	bravely	hill
hungry	~~slowly~~	horse	by

Adjective	Noun	Preposition	Adverb
heavy	table	over	slowly

/4

5. The passage below is missing some punctuation. Write out the passage on the lines, adding in the correct punctuation.

> charlotte said to her mother I LOVE cats please please please can I have one charlotte's mother told her she could have a cat if she was able to look after it herself Charlotte was determined to prove that she would be a good cat owner

_____

_____

_____

_____

_____

/6

Score:		Time taken:		Target met?	

Target time: **12 minutes**

1. Underline the word in each set of brackets that is closest in meaning to the word in bold.

    Example: cold   (hot <u>chilly</u> dry)

    a) **centre**   (middle   end   edge)

    b) **possess**   (lose   own   find)

    c) **location**   (look   position   date)

    d) **enough**   (plenty   little   though)

    /4

2. Decide which of the words in bold is the correct word for each sentence. Underline the word.

    Example: I watched the **plain / <u>plane</u>** take off.

    a) I didn't mean to **break / brake** the glass.

    b) Polly was proud when she learnt to **so / sew**.

    c) **Where / Wear** are you going later?

    d) There was a hole in the **soul / sole** of his boot.

    /4

3. One word from the first set of brackets goes together with one word from the second set of brackets to make a new word. Underline the two words and write the new word on the line.

    Example: (<u>tooth</u> mouth nose)   (pen <u>brush</u> pencil)   <u>toothbrush</u>

    a) (there here over)   (for fore four)   _____

    b) (clock watch time)   (chair table seat)   _____

    c) (life love laugh)   (happy grin line)   _____

    d) (stars sun hot)   (rain snow light)   _____

    /4

4. Write out the words in each row on the line so that they are in alphabetical order.

Example: duck cat dog fox   <u>cat dog duck fox</u>

a) leaf twig branch trunk

_____

b) van coach car truck

_____

c) clip clap crow creep

_____

d) feed free feather fire

_____

/4

5. The passage below contains <u>six</u> spelling errors. Find each word that is spelt incorrectly, underline it and then write the correct spelling on the line.

My favurite type of food is ice cream. I love the smooth, creamy sensashun as the ice cream touches my tonge. I enjoy every kind of ice cream, but the best flavur of all is chocolate chip. I am also quite partial to a big bowl of delishus rasberry ripple. If I had my way, I would eat ice cream for every meal: breakfast, lunch and dinner!

_____   _____

_____   _____

_____   _____

/6

Score:		Time taken:		Target met?	

Progress chart

Write the score (out of 22) for each test in the box provided on the right of the graph.
Then colour in the row next to the box to represent this score.

Section 1

		Total
Test 1		
Test 2		
Test 3		
Test 4		
Test 5		
Test 6		

1 2 3 4 5 6 7 8 9 10 11 12 13 14 15 16 17 18 19 20 21 22

Score (out of 22)

Section 2

		Total
Test 1		
Test 2		
Test 3		
Test 4		
Test 5		
Test 6		

1 2 3 4 5 6 7 8 9 10 11 12 13 14 15 16 17 18 19 20 21 22

Score (out of 22)

Section 3

		Total
Test 1		
Test 2		
Test 3		
Test 4		
Test 5		
Test 6		

1 2 3 4 5 6 7 8 9 10 11 12 13 14 15 16 17 18 19 20 21 22

Score (out of 22)